AF504388

"For the beginning gardener, Dick Nasca's newest children's book, Victory Garden, is a real treasure. Both you and your inquisitive youngster will together enjoy its informative and well-presented contents. Many colorful illustrations throughout add depth to the simple story, while common gardening terms and easy-to-follow instructions are included, all offered by a lifetime Master Gardener."
Ed Hearn

"This book is well written for young readers and the artwork is most appealing, which truly makes the book meaningful."
W. Jack Bostrom

"When I saw your book, I was very impressed. Your combination of cartoons and text are very impressive. All young readers will be your fans. Well done."
André Brillaud

Victory Garden
Grow Your Own Food

By Richard J. Nasca M.D.
Illustrated by Chris Fowler

Published by IngramSpark

Dedication

To all those who labor to grow their own vegetables year after year.

Foreword

During the Second World War, World War II, because of a shortage of food, it was necessary for people to grow their own vegetables. These gardens were given the name, Victory Gardens. Victory Gardens were planted by families in their yards and the vegetables were stored in glass jars for use later by a process called canning.

In order to buy meat, sugar and other items which were rationed, it was necessary to have food tokens. After the war, people continued to plant gardens and can or freeze the vegetables for use during the winter.

The purpose of this story, which is true, is to entertain children and encourage them to grow a garden. Not only will they enjoy the process of growing things, but they will learn how to care for their plants and experience the joy of harvesting their own home-grown vegetables.

Ritchie was six when he dug his first Victory Garden in the small yard in the back of his house.

Ritchie had no tools, so his friend Ernie brought him a rake, shovel, pitchfork and small metal hoe that belonged to his sister, Gail.

Ernie and his four sisters had planted their
Victory Garden next door in their backyard.

Ritchie had a difficult time digging up the hard red clay, so his neighbor Frank came over to help him.

Richie and Frank were admiring their work when the air raid sirens went off. Everyone ran up to the Air Raid Shelter in the basement of an apartment building at the end of the street.

Ritchie's father was an Air Raid warden and guided people into the shelter with tables and cots lined up in the basement of the apartment.

Ritchie joined his mother and baby sister, Gerry, in the shelter. After the all-clear siren, they returned home to eat their dinner in the dark kitchen with the window shades down.

The next day, Ritchie got up early to finish digging the little backyard garden and breakup the clods of clay with the little hoe.

Ernie's sister, Gail, was looking down on
Ritchie from her back porch as he
was using her hoe.

Gail ran over to Ritchie's yard and said, "I want my hoe back now. My brother had no right to lend you my hoe." She grabbed it out of his hand and hit him on the bridge of his nose with the sharp end of the hoe.

Ritchie was taken to the hospital for treatment bleeding from the outside and inside of his nose.

A week later, Ritchie ventured out into his freshly dug plot using his own new little rake, shovel and hoe to plant his garden and Gail came to apologize.

He planted little radish seeds, carrots, beets, and lettuce.

He used a little tin can to water his garden each day.

A few weeks later, his mother bought him three little tomato plants which he added to his garden.

Every few days, Ritchie would pull
weeds from around his plants.

After six weeks, he started picking lettuce
and little red radishes that he brought to his
mother to make salad.

Later, the carrots and beets were ready to pull up from their home in the ground.

On July 4th, Ritchie picked his first tomato.

His mother cut the tomato into slices and
made lettuce, bacon and tomato sandwiches

By early August, the little garden was full of bright red tomatoes and little rows of lettuce and radishes.

Gardening Terms

Seeds: Small grains that grow into new plants.

Pot: A small container filled with soil in which seeds are planted.

Nursery: A warm room with lots of windows where newly planted seeds are placed to grow into seedlings.

Seedlings: Small new plants.

Minerals: Found naturally in soil, they serve as food for plants and are necessary for plant growth. Examples of minerals are nitrogen, phosphorus and potassium.

Stem: The main support for the plant, similar to the trunk of a tree.

Branches: Also called vines, they extend from the stem and provide support for the leaves, fruits and vegetables.

Leaves: Flat, thin and usually green in color, they provide nutrients to fruits, vegetables and flowers.

Roots: A group of many thin stems that grow underground to support the plant and provide it with water and minerals.

Pollinate: The act of taking pollen (plant dust) from the flower of one plant and placing it onto another plant to help it grow.

Hornworm: A type of worm that eats the stems and leaves of a plant and can cause it to die.

Soapy Liquid: Used to stop insects and other plant diseases, this combination of soap, oil and water does not hurt the plant.

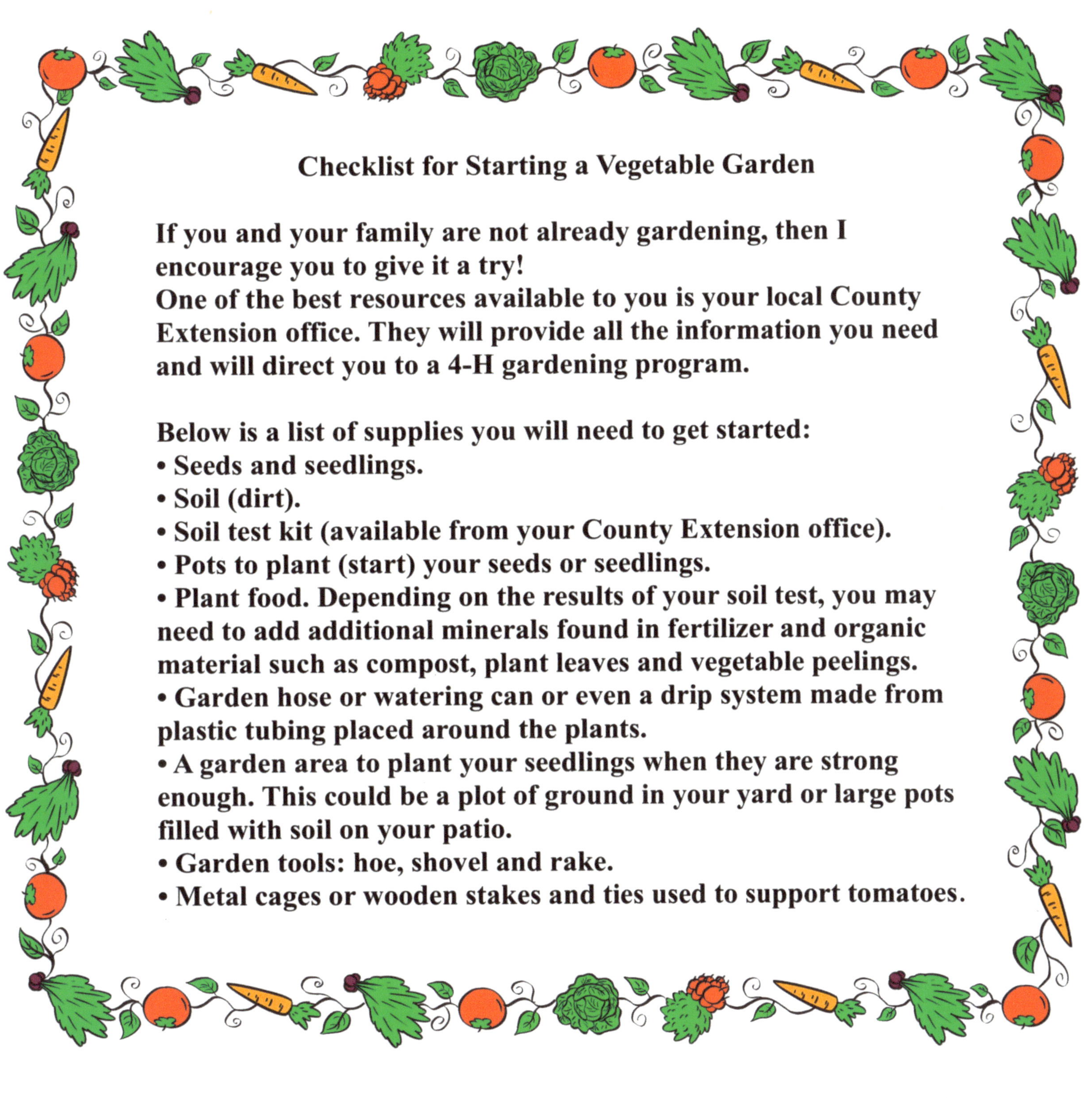

Checklist for Starting a Vegetable Garden

If you and your family are not already gardening, then I encourage you to give it a try!
One of the best resources available to you is your local County Extension office. They will provide all the information you need and will direct you to a 4-H gardening program.

Below is a list of supplies you will need to get started:
• Seeds and seedlings.
• Soil (dirt).
• Soil test kit (available from your County Extension office).
• Pots to plant (start) your seeds or seedlings.
• Plant food. Depending on the results of your soil test, you may need to add additional minerals found in fertilizer and organic material such as compost, plant leaves and vegetable peelings.
• Garden hose or watering can or even a drip system made from plastic tubing placed around the plants.
• A garden area to plant your seedlings when they are strong enough. This could be a plot of ground in your yard or large pots filled with soil on your patio.
• Garden tools: hoe, shovel and rake.
• Metal cages or wooden stakes and ties used to support tomatoes.

Timeframe

It is important to plant each vegetable at the right time. Some grow in cool weather whereas others thrive in warm weather. Because the United States is such a large country, it has different climate zones, which means that it is colder in some places than others at the same time of year.

Thus, you need to research the best time to plant particular vegetables in your area. You can contact your local County Extension office for this information or check the back of the seed packets.

In general, once planted in pots, it can take 4-5 weeks for your seeds to grow into seedlings strong enough to be transplanted into the garden.

It will then take another 2-3 months (or longer) before your vegetables are fully grown and ready to eat.

About the author

Richard J. Nasca, MD, is a retired orthopaedic and spine surgeon who has enjoyed growing vegetables since his first Victory Garden in 1944 on a small plot in his backyard in Washington, DC. He is a certified Master Gardener living in Wilmington, NC and hopes that *Victory Garden* will motivate children to garden. Since he retired, he has written the following children's books that your children may wish to read. They are available on amazon.com.

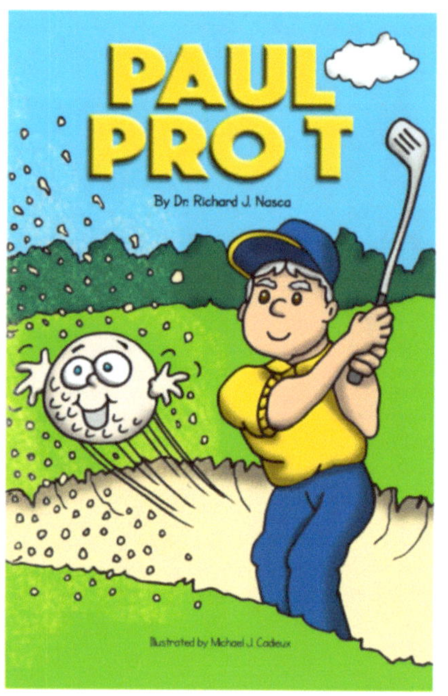

Paul Pro T is an illustrated story about the highs and lows of the game of golf as told by Paul Pro T, a golf ball. Written for children ages 5-10. The book includes a glossary of terms and tips on how to get started playing golf.

Billy Bluebird is an illustrated book about the life cycle of bluebirds Billy and Bonnie and their newly born offspring. The book is written for children ages 4–10 and contains plans and instructions on building a bluebird house.

Tommy Tomato is an illustrated story that entertains and educates children ages 5–10 as they learn how to successfully grow a tomato. The book includes a helpful checklist and definitions of gardening terms.

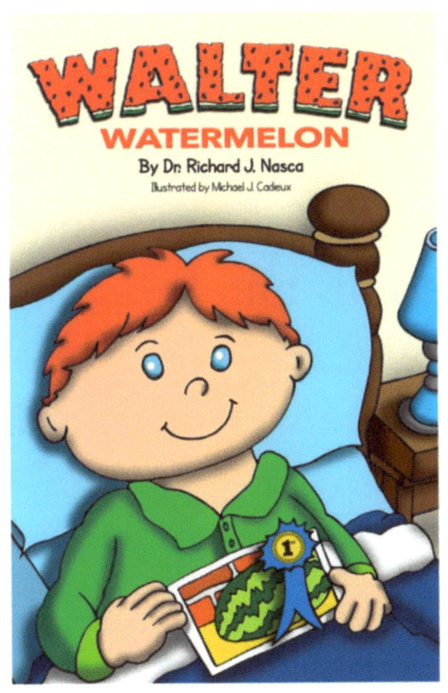

Walter Watermelon is an illustrated story that is written to both entertain and educate children ages 4–8. The book includes helpful information about starting and maintaining a garden, as well as commonly used gardening terms, to encourage children to discover the joys of growing their own vegetables.

About the illustrator

Hailing from Wilmington, North Carolina, Chris Fowler seeks to captivate young minds with his enchanting illustrations. With a portfolio of several illustrated books, he focuses on the magic of being a kid, igniting children's imaginations and fostering understanding. His art creates joyful connections for families, inviting them to explore the wonders of his fun field books.